HAL•LEONARD

UKULELE PLAY-ALONG

AUDIO ACCESS INCLUDED

PLAYBACK+
Speed • Pitch • Balance • Loop

VOL. 36

ELVIS Presley
Hawaii

T0085310

To access audio visit:
www.halleonard.com/mylibrary

Enter Code
5625-9174-3925-7037

Ukulele by Chris Kringel

Cover photo © Elvis Presley Enterprises

Elvis and Elvis Presley are registered trademarks of Elvis Presley Enterprise, Inc.
Copyright © 2015

ISBN 978-1-4950-0237-3

HAL•LEONARD®
CORPORATION

7777 W. BLUEMOUND RD. P.O. BOX 13819 MILWAUKEE, WI 53213

www.elvis.com

Visit Hal Leonard Online at
www.halleonard.com

UKULELE NOTATION LEGEND

THE MUSICAL STAFF shows pitches and rhythms and is divided by bar lines into measures. Pitches are named after the first seven letters of the alphabet.

TABLATURE graphically represents the ukulele fingerboard. Each horizontal line represents a a string, and each number represents a fret.

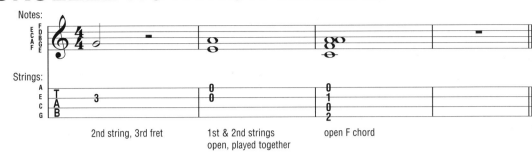

2nd string, 3rd fret

1st & 2nd strings open, played together

open F chord

HALF-STEP BEND: Strike the note and bend up 1/2 step.

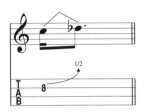

WHOLE-STEP BEND: Strike the note and bend up one step.

GRACE NOTE BEND: Strike the note and immediately bend up as indicated.

SLIGHT (MICROTONE) BEND: Strike the note and bend up 1/4 step.

BEND AND RELEASE: Strike the note and bend up as indicated, then release back to the original note. Only the first note is struck.

PRE-BEND: Bend the note as indicated, then strike it.

VIBRATO: The string is vibrated by rapidly bending and releasing the note with the fretting hand.

HAMMER-ON: Strike the first (lower) note with one finger, then sound the higher note (on the same string) with another finger by fretting it without picking.

PULL-OFF: Place both fingers on the notes to be sounded. Strike the first note and without picking, pull the finger off to sound the second (lower) note.

LEGATO SLIDE: Strike the first note and then slide the same fret-hand finger up or down to the second note. The second note is not struck.

SHIFT SLIDE: Same as legato slide, except the second note is struck.

TRILL: Very rapidly alternate between the notes indicated by continuously hammering on and pulling off.

TREMOLO PICKING: The note is picked as rapidly and continuously as possible.

NOTE: Tablature numbers in parentheses mean:

1. The note is being sustained over a system (note in standard notation is tied), or

2. The note is sustained, but a new articulation (such as a hammer-on, pull-off, slide or vibrato) begins, or

3. The note is a barely audible "ghost" note (note in standard notation is also in parentheses).

Additional Musical Definitions

(accent)

- Accentuate note (play it louder)

(staccato)

- Play the note short

D.S. al Coda

- Go back to the sign (%), then play until the measure marked "**To Coda**," then skip to the section labelled "**Coda**."

D.C. al Fine

- Go back to the beginning of the song and play until the measure marked "*Fine*" (end).

N.C.

- No chord.

- Repeat measures between signs.

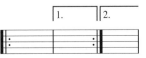

- When a repeated section has different endings, play the first ending only the first time and the second ending only the second time.

CONTENTS

Aloha Oe

Words and Music by Queen Liliuokalani

First note

Intro
Freely
*Em

Saxophone   **Vocal

*Trem. pick till Chorus.   **Hawaiian lyrics not available.

Saxophone

Vocal

Saxophone

Ha - a -

Slow ♩ = 65

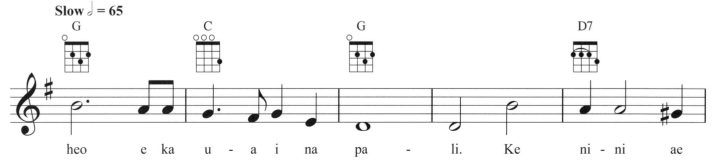

heo   e   ka   u - a - i   na   pa -   li.   Ke   ni - ni   ae

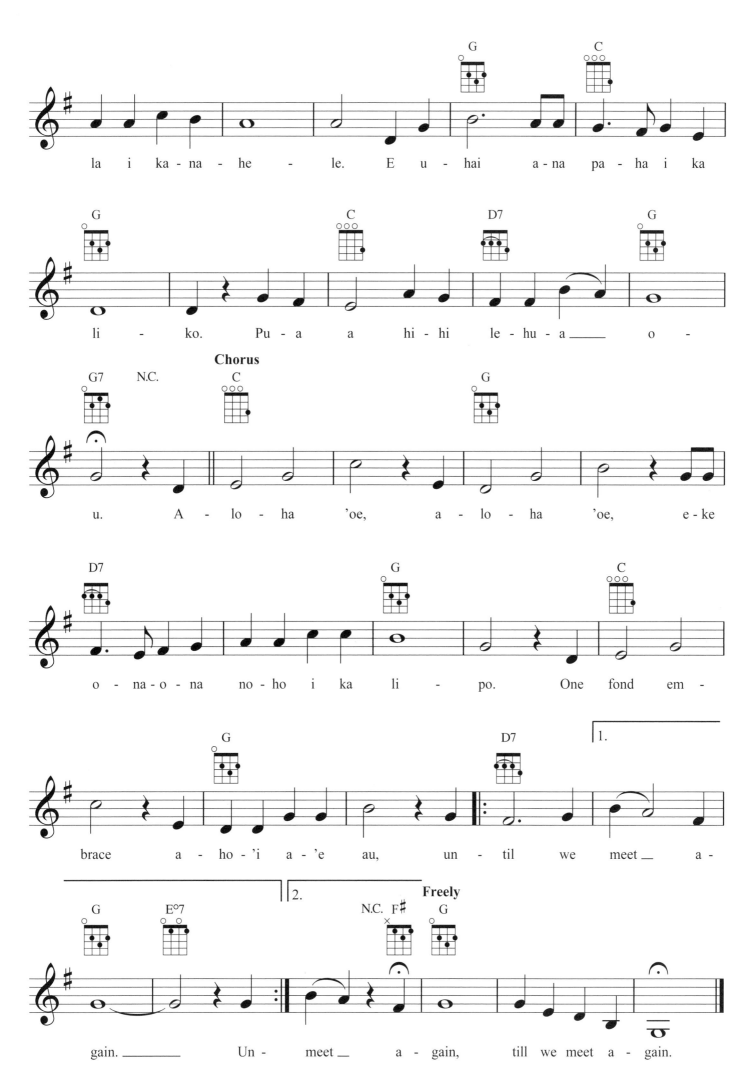

Blue Hawaii

from the Paramount Picture WAIKIKI WEDDING

Words and Music by Leo Robin and Ralph Rainger

Can't Help Falling in Love

from the Paramount Picture BLUE HAWAII

Words and Music by George David Weiss, Hugo Peretti and Luigi Creatore

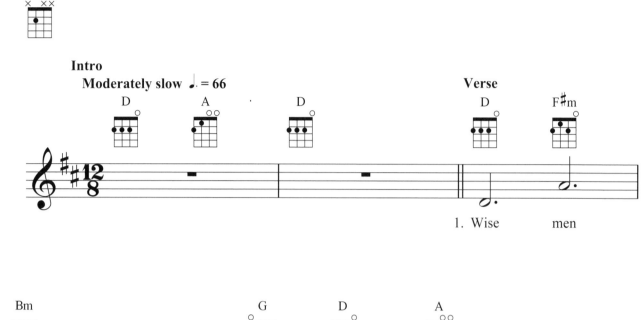

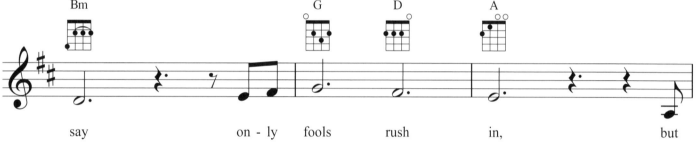

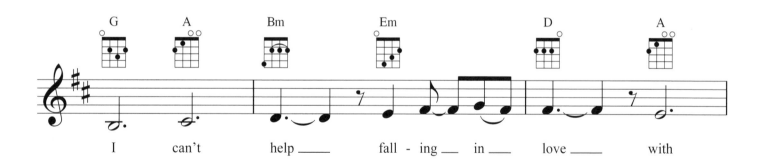

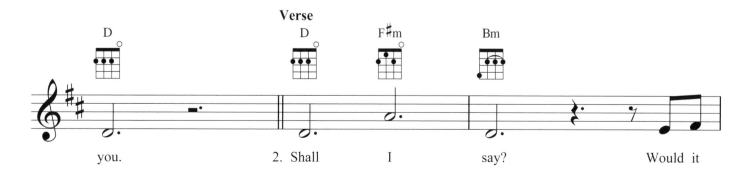

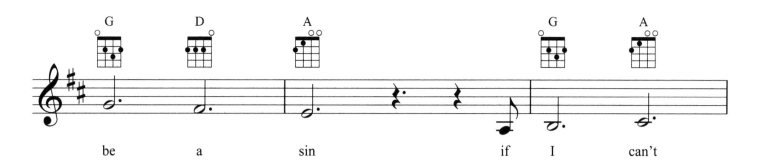

be   a   sin   if   I   can't

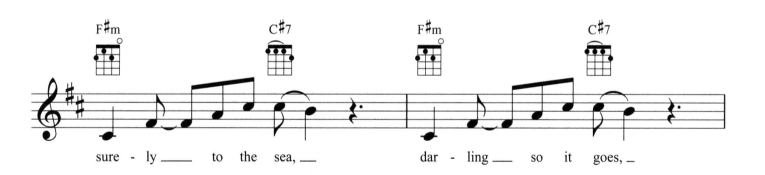

help _____ fall - ing ____ in _____ love _____ with

Bridge

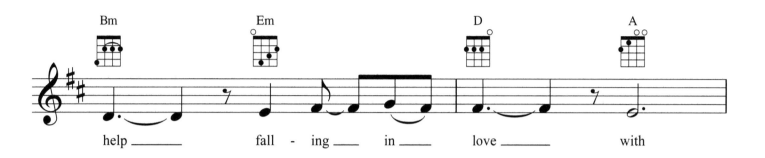

you?   Like   a _____ riv - er   flows __

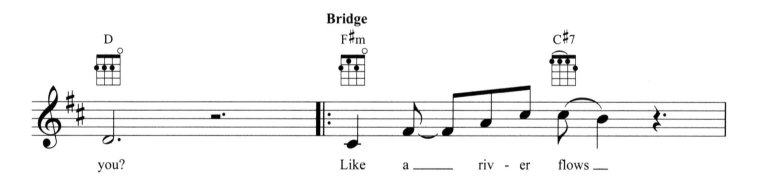

sure - ly _____ to   the   sea, __   dar - ling ___ so   it   goes, __

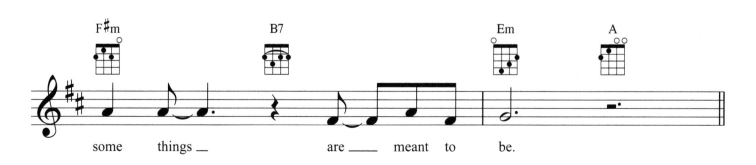

some   things ___   are ____ meant   to   be.

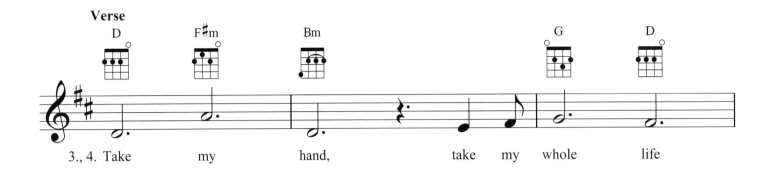

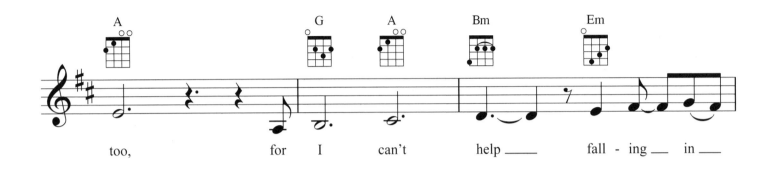

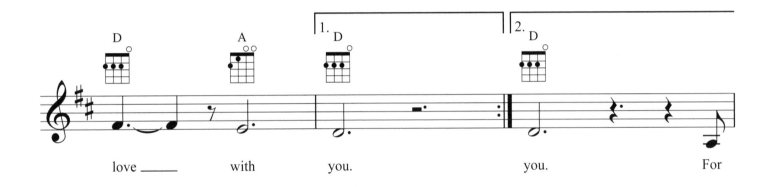

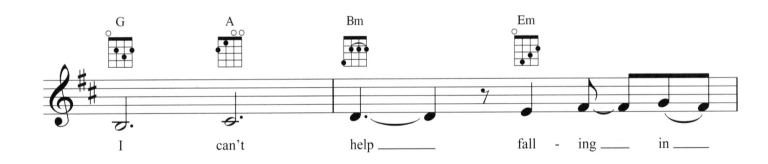

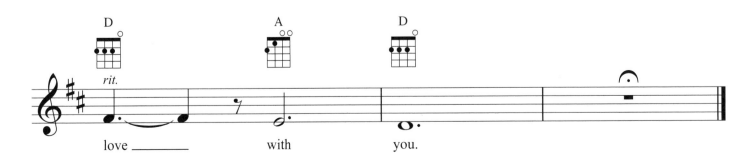

The Hawaiian Wedding Song
(Ke Kali Nei Au)

English Lyrics by Al Hoffman and Dick Manning
Hawaiian Lyrics and Music by Charles E. King

*Hawaiian lyrics not available.

Verse

3. Ko a-lo-ha ma - Ka-mea e i - po.

Ka - 'u ia e le - i a e ne - i la.

Now ___ that we are ___ one, clouds won't hide ___ the

Outro

sun. Blue _ skies ___ of Ha - wa - ii smile on

this, ___ our wed-ding ___ day I do ___ love ___

rit.

you ___ with all my ___ heart.

Love Me

Words and Music by Jerry Leiber and Mike Stoller

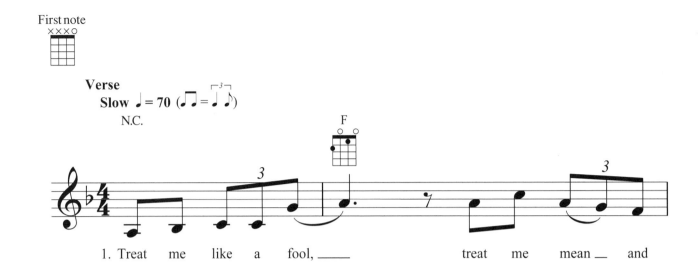

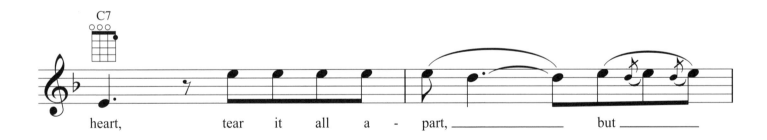

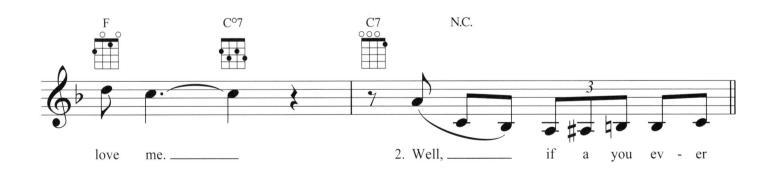

Verse

(3.) go, _____ dar - lin', I'll _____ be, oh, _____ so _____

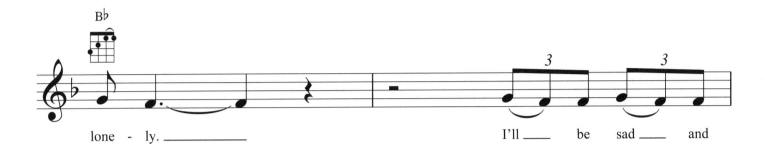

lone - ly. _____ I'll _____ be sad _____ and

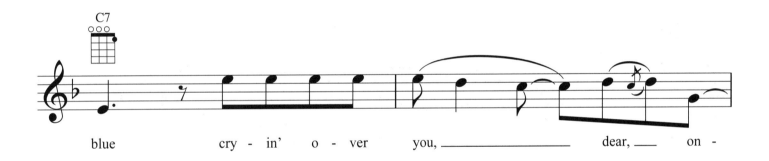

blue cry - in' o - ver you, _____ dear, _____ on -

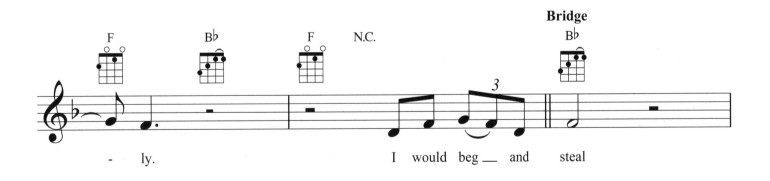

Bridge

- ly. I would beg _____ and steal

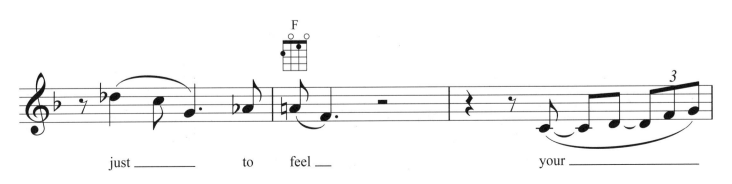

just _____ to feel _____ your _____

heart _____ beat - ing close to ____

mine. _____ 3., 4. Well, __ if a you ev - er

Verse

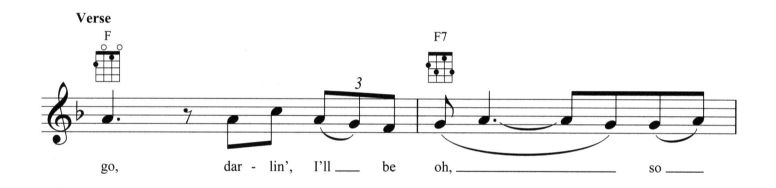

go, dar - lin', I'll __ be oh, _____ so ____

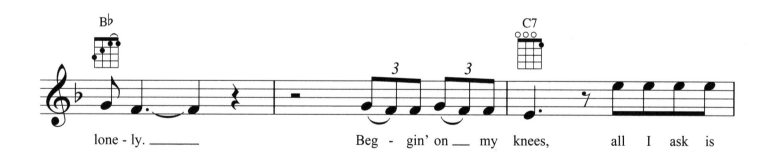

lone - ly. _____ Beg - gin' on __ my knees, all I ask is

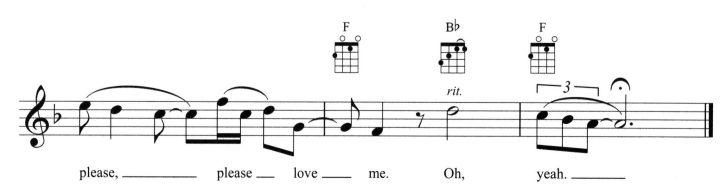

please, _____ please __ love __ me. Oh, yeah.

Moonlight Swim

Words and Music by Sylvia Dee and Ben Weisman

Verse

moon - light swim. To the raft we can race and for

just a lit - tle while ___ I'll sit and pre - tend that you're

on a des - ert isle with me on a moon - light swim.

Bridge

Though the air is cold, with kis - ses oh so

sweet I'll keep you warm so ve - ry warm, ___

from your head to your feet. _____ 3., 4. Let's go on a

moon - light swim. We're in love and a - bove there's a

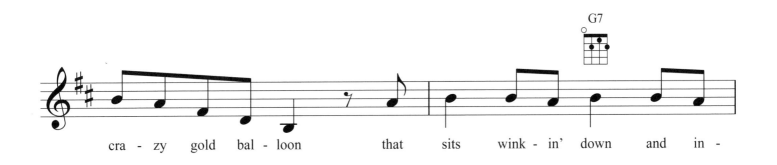

cra - zy gold bal - loon that sits wink - in' down and in -

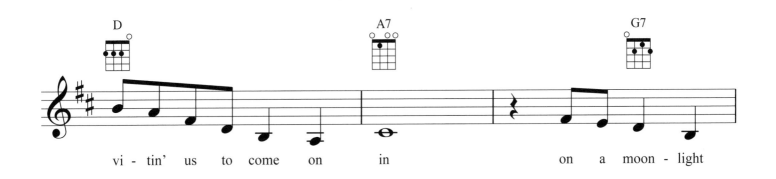

vi - tin' us to come on in on a moon - light

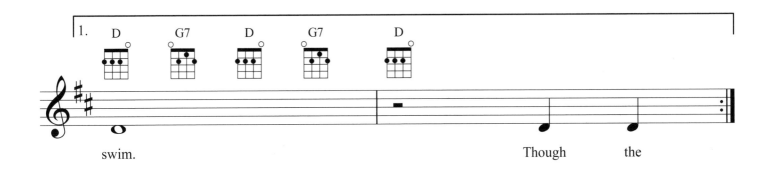

swim. Though the

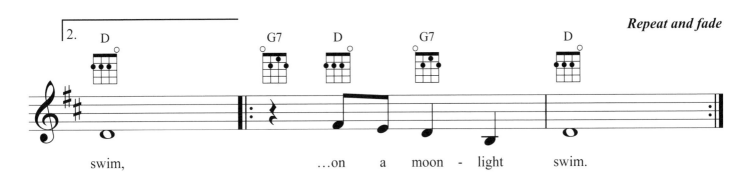

swim, ...on a moon - light swim.

My Way

English Words by Paul Anka
Original French Words by Gilles Thibault
Music by Jacques Revaux and Claude Francois

friend, I'll say it clear, I'll state my case, of which I'm
did what I had to do, and saw it through with - out ex -
now, as tears sub - side, I find it all so a -

cer - tain. I've lived a life that's full I trav - eled
emp - tion. I planned each chart - ed course, each care - ful
mus - ing to think I did all that, and may I

each and ev - 'ry high - way, and more, much more than
step a - long the by - way, and more, much more than
say, not in a shy way. Oh, no, oh, no, not

To Coda

1.

2.

this, I did it my way. 2. Re - way. Yes, there were
this, I did it my
me, I did it my

Chorus

times, I'm sure you knew, when I bit off more than I could

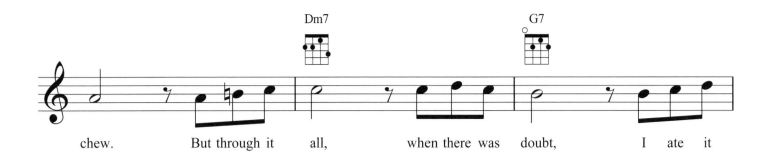

chew.   But through it   all,   when there was   doubt,   I ate it

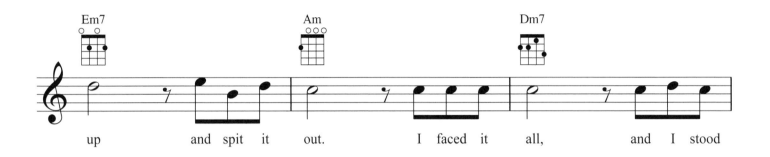

up   and spit it out.   I faced it   all,   and I stood

D.S. al Coda

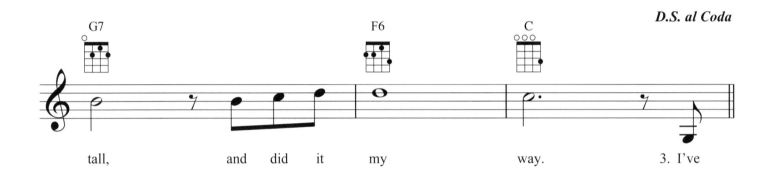

tall,   and did it my   way.   3. I've

Coda

Chorus
Faster ♩. = 92

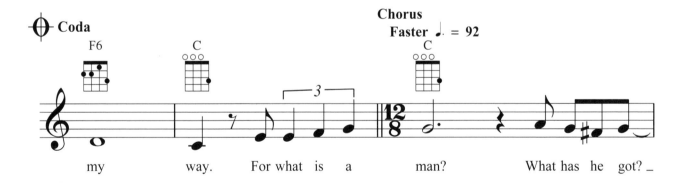

my   way.   For what is a   man?   What has he got? _

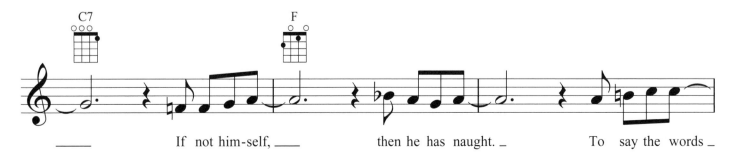

____   If not him-self, ___   then he has naught. _   To say the words _

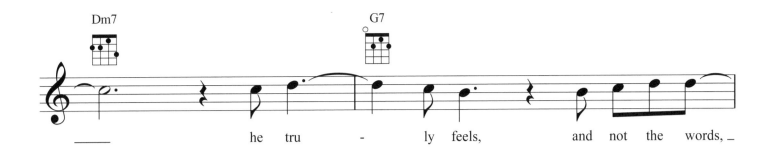

he tru - ly feels, and not the words, _

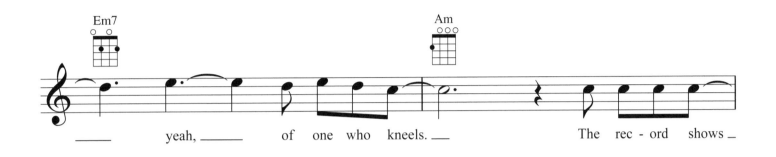

_ yeah, _ of one who kneels. _ The rec - ord shows _

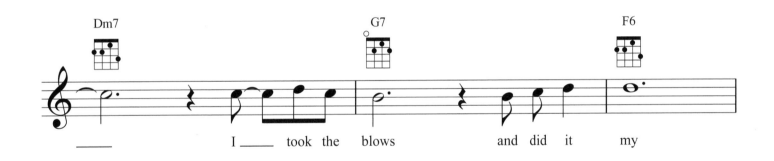

_ I _ took the blows and did it my

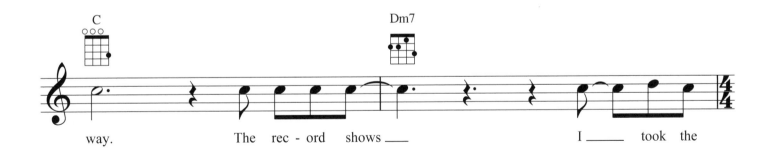

way. The rec - ord shows _ I _ took the

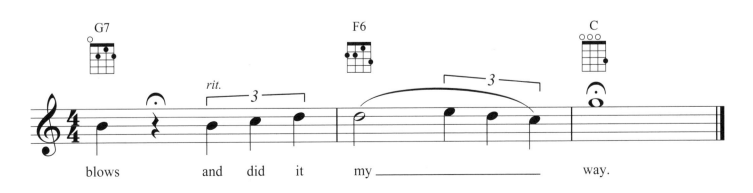

blows and did it my _ way.

Rock-A-Hula Baby

Words and Music by Fred Wise, Ben Weisman and Dolores Fuller

rock, a - hu - la rock, a - hu - la ra! 1. The way she

Verse

moves her hips — up to her fin - ger - tips, — I feel I'm hea - ven bound. —

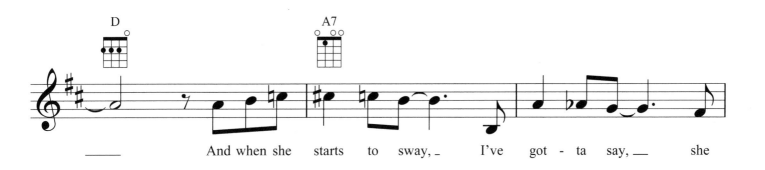

— And when she starts to sway, — I've got - ta say, — she

Chorus

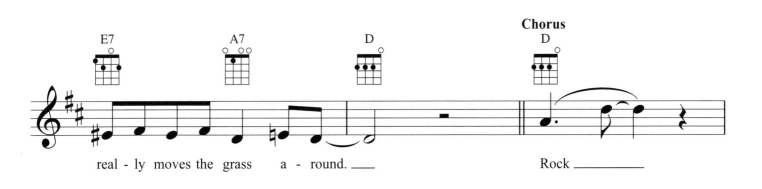

real - ly moves the grass a - round. — Rock —

a - hu - la ba - by, rock, — a - hu - la ba - by. Got - ta

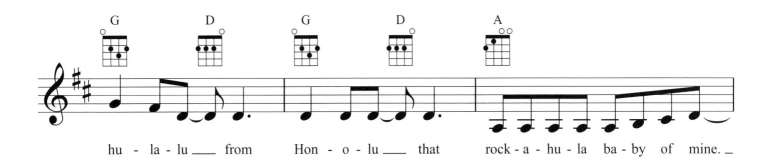

hu - la - lu __ from Hon - o - lu __ that rock - a - hu - la ba - by of mine. __

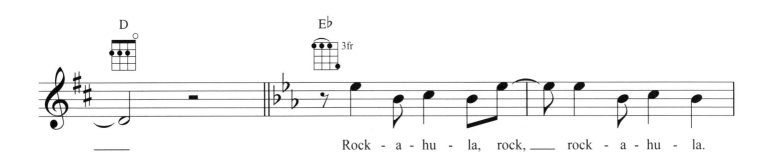

__ Rock - a - hu - la, rock, __ rock - a - hu - la.

Verse

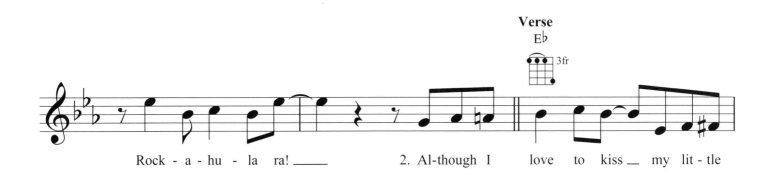

Rock - a - hu - la ra! __ 2. Al - though I love to kiss __ my lit - tle

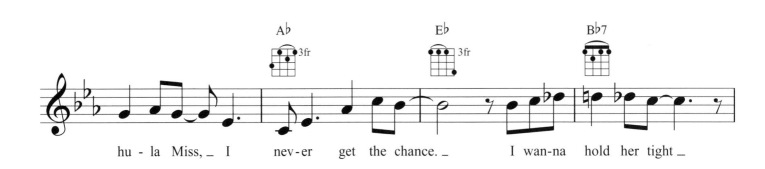

hu - la Miss, __ I nev - er get the chance. __ I wan - na hold her tight __

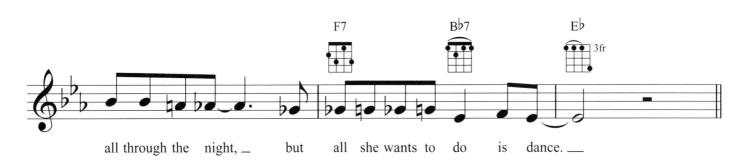

all through the night, __ but all she wants to do is dance. __

Chorus

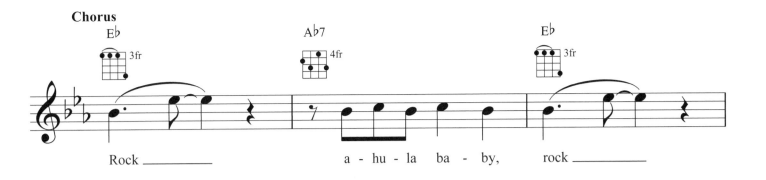

Rock _____ a - hu - la ba - by, rock _____

a - hu - la ba - by. Got - ta hu - la lu __ from Hon - o - lu __ that

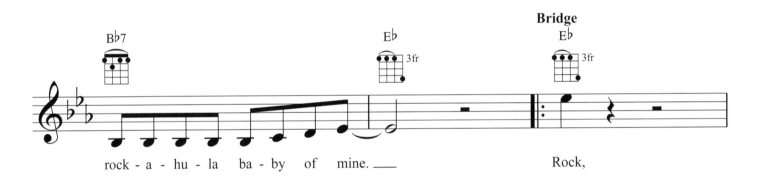

rock - a - hu - la ba - by of mine. __ Rock,

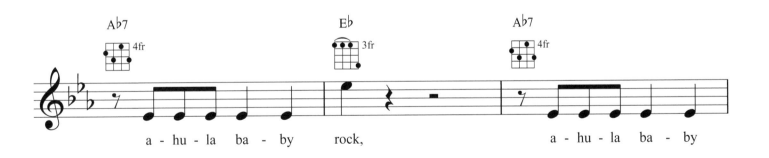

a - hu - la ba - by rock, a - hu - la ba - by

rock, a - hu - la ba - by. Rock, rock, rock, rock!

Chorus

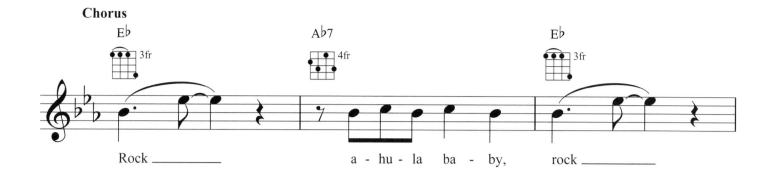

Rock _____ a - hu - la ba - by, rock _____

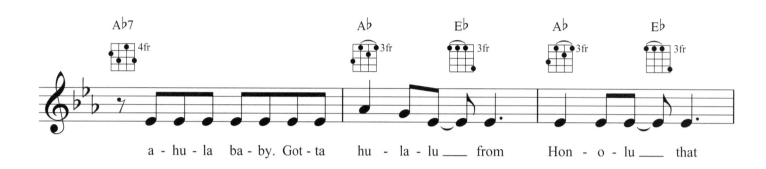

a - hu - la ba - by. Got - ta hu - la - lu ___ from Hon - o - lu ___ that

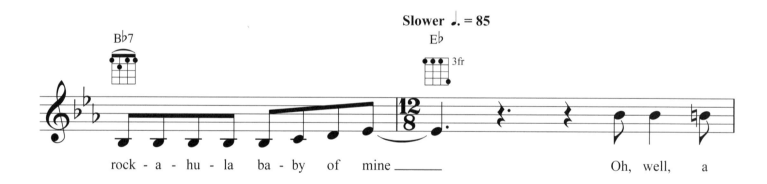

rock - a - hu - la ba - by of mine _____ Oh, well, a

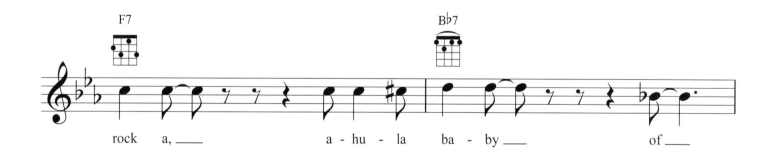

rock a, ___ a - hu - la ba - by ___ of ___

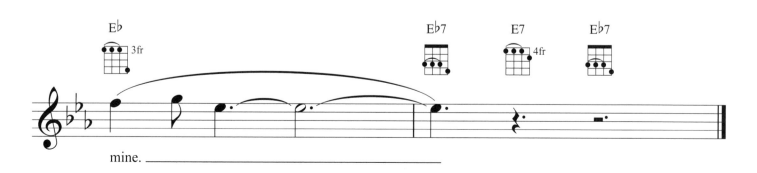

mine. _____

HAL·LEONARD UKULELE PLAY-ALONG®

Now you can play your favorite songs on your uke with great-sounding backing tracks to help you sound like a bona fide pro! This series includes the Amazing Slow Downer, so you can adjust the tempo without changing the pitch by using the CD in your computer.

1. POP HITS
00701451 Book/CD Pack.........................$14.99

2. UKE CLASSICS
00701452 Book/CD Pack.........................$12.99

3. HAWAIIAN FAVORITES
00701453 Book/CD Pack.........................$12.99

4. CHILDREN'S SONGS
00701454 Book/CD Pack.........................$12.99

5. CHRISTMAS SONGS
00701696 Book/CD Pack.........................$12.99

6. LENNON & McCARTNEY
00701723 Book/CD Pack.........................$12.99

7. DISNEY FAVORITES
00701724 Book/CD Pack.........................$12.99

8. CHART HITS
00701745 Book/CD Pack.........................$14.99

9. THE SOUND OF MUSIC
00701784 Book/CD Pack.........................$12.99

10. MOTOWN
00701964 Book/CD Pack.........................$12.99

11. CHRISTMAS STRUMMING
00702458 Book/CD Pack.........................$12.99

12. BLUEGRASS FAVORITES
00702584 Book/CD Pack.........................$12.99

13. UKULELE SONGS
00702599 Book/CD Pack.........................$12.99

14. JOHNNY CASH
00702615 Book/CD Pack.........................$14.99

15. COUNTRY CLASSICS
00702834 Book/CD Pack.........................$12.99

16. STANDARDS
00702835 Book/CD Pack.........................$12.99

17. POP STANDARDS
00702836 Book/CD Pack.........................$12.99

18. IRISH SONGS
00703086 Book/CD Pack.........................$12.99

19. BLUES STANDARDS
00703087 Book/CD Pack.........................$12.99

20. FOLK POP ROCK
00703088 Book/CD Pack.........................$12.99

21. HAWAIIAN CLASSICS
00703097 Book/CD Pack.........................$12.99

22. ISLAND SONGS
00703098 Book/CD Pack.........................$12.99

23. TAYLOR SWIFT
00704106 Book/CD Pack.........................$14.99

24. WINTER WONDERLAND
00101871 Book/CD Pack.........................$12.99

25. GREEN DAY
00110398 Book/CD Pack.........................$14.99

26. BOB MARLEY
00110399 Book/CD Pack.........................$14.99

27. TIN PAN ALLEY
00116358 Book/CD Pack.........................$12.99

28. STEVIE WONDER
00116736 Book/CD Pack.........................$14.99

29. OVER THE RAINBOW & OTHER FAVORITES
00117076 Book/CD Pack.........................$14.99

30. ACOUSTIC SONGS
00122336 Book/CD Pack.........................$14.99

31. JASON MRAZ
00124166 Book/CD Pack.........................$14.99

32. TOP DOWNLOADS
00127507 Book/CD Pack.........................$14.99

34. CHRISTMAS HITS
00128602 Book/CD Pack.........................$14.99

36. ELVIS PRESLEY HAWAII
00138199 Book/CD Pack.........................$14.99

HAL·LEONARD® CORPORATION

7777 W. BLUEMOUND RD. P.O. BOX 13819 MILWAUKEE, WI 53213

www.halleonard.com

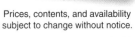

Prices, contents, and availability subject to change without notice.

0515

Ride the Ukulele Wave!

The Beach Boys for Ukulele

This folio features 20 favorites, including: Barbara Ann • Be True to Your School • California Girls • Fun, Fun, Fun • God Only Knows • Good Vibrations • Help Me Rhonda • I Get Around • In My Room • Kokomo • Little Deuce Coupe • Sloop John B • Surfin' U.S.A. • Wouldn't It Be Nice • and more!

00701726 . . . .$14.99

The Beatles for Ukulele

Ukulele players can strum, sing and pick along with 20 Beatles classics! Includes: All You Need Is Love • Eight Days a Week • Good Day Sunshine • Here, There and Everywhere • Let It Be • Love Me Do • Penny Lane • Yesterday • and more.

00700154 . . . .$16.99

The Daily Ukulele

compiled and arranged by
Liz and Jim Beloff
Strum a different song everyday with easy arrangements of 365 of your favorite songs in one big songbook! Includes favorites by the Beatles, Beach Boys, and Bob Dylan, folk songs, pop songs, kids' songs, Christmas carols, and Broadway and Hollywood tunes, all with a spiral binding for ease of use.

00240356 . . . .$34.99

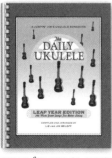

The Daily Ukulele – Leap Year Edition

366 More Songs for Better Living
compiled and arranged by
Liz and Jim Beloff
An amazing second volume with 366 MORE songs for you to master each day of a leap year! Includes: Ain't No Sunshine • Calendar Girl • I Got You Babe • Lean on Me • Moondance • and many, many more.

00240681 . . . .$34.99

Disney Songs for Ukulele

20 great Disney classics arranged for all uke players, including: Beauty and the Beast • Bibbidi-Bobbidi-Boo (The Magic Song) • Can You Feel the Love Tonight • Chim Chim Cher-ee • Heigh-Ho • It's a Small World • Some Day My Prince Will Come • We're All in This Together • When You Wish upon a Star • and more.

00701708 . . . .$12.99

Folk Songs for Ukulele

A great collection to take along to the campfire! 60 folk songs, including: Amazing Grace • Buffalo Gals • Camptown Races • For He's a Jolly Good Fellow • Good Night Ladies • Home on the Range • I've Been Working on the Railroad • Kumbaya • My Bonnie Lies over the Ocean • On Top of Old Smoky • Scarborough Fair • Swing Low, Sweet Chariot • Take Me Out to the Ball Game • Yankee Doodle • and more.

00696068 . . . .$12.99

Glee

Music from the Fox Television Show for Ukulele
20 favorites for Gleeks to strum and sing, including: Bad Romance • Beautiful • Defying Gravity • Don't Stop Believin' • No Air • Proud Mary • Rehab • True Colors • and more.

00701722 . . . .$14.99

Hawaiian Songs for Ukulele

Over thirty songs from the state that made the ukulele famous, including: Beyond the Rainbow • Hanalei Moon • Ka-lu-a • Lovely Hula Girl • Mele Kalikimaka • One More Aloha • Sea Breeze • Tiny Bubbles • Waikiki • and more.

00696065 . . . .$9.99

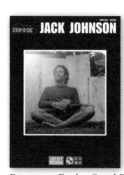

Jack Johnson – Strum & Sing

Cherry Lane Music
Strum along with 41 Jack Johnson songs using this top-notch collection of chords and lyrics just for the uke! Includes: Better Together • Bubble Toes • Cocoon • Do You Remember • Flake • Fortunate Fool • Good People • Holes to Heaven • Taylor • Tomorrow Morning • and more.

02501702 . . . .$15.99

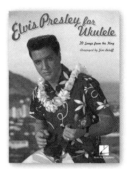

Elvis Presley for Ukulele

arr. Jim Beloff
20 classic hits from The King: All Shook Up • Blue Hawaii • Blue Suede Shoes • Can't Help Falling in Love • Don't • Heartbreak Hotel • Hound Dog • Jailhouse Rock • Love Me • Love Me Tender • Return to Sender • Suspicious Minds • Teddy Bear • and more.

00701004 . . . .$14.99

Jake Shimabukuro – Peace Love Ukulele

Deemed "the Hendrix of the ukulele," Hawaii native Jake Shimabukuro is a uke virtuoso. Our songbook features note-for-note transcriptions with ukulele tablature of Jake's masterful playing on all the CD tracks: Bohemian Rhapsody • Boy Meets Girl • Bring Your Adz • Hallelujah • Pianoforte 2010 • Variation on a Dance 2010 • and more, plus two bonus selections!

00702516 . . . .$19.99

Worship Songs for Ukulele

25 worship songs: Amazing Grace (My Chains are Gone) • Blessed Be Your Name • Enough • God of Wonders • Holy Is the Lord • How Great Is Our God • In Christ Alone • Love the Lord • Mighty to Save • Sing to the King • Step by Step • We Fall Down • and more.

00702546 . . . .$12.99

HAL•LEONARD® CORPORATION
7777 W. BLUEMOUND RD. P.O. BOX 13819 MILWAUKEE, WI 53213

UKULELE ENSEMBLE SERIES

The songs in these collections are playable by any combination of ukuleles (soprano, concert, tenor or baritone). Each arrangement features the melody, a harmony part, and a "bass" line. Chord symbols are also provided if you wish to add a rhythm part. For groups with more than three or four ukuleles, the parts may be doubled.

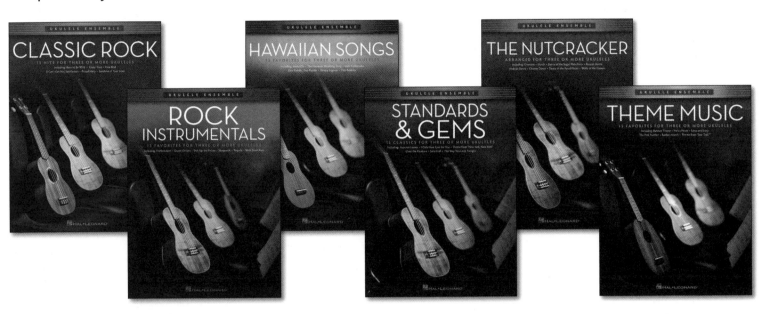

CHRISTMAS CAROLS
Early Intermediate Level

Away in a Manger • Carol of the Bells • Deck the Hall • The First Noel • God Rest Ye Merry, Gentlemen • Hark! the Herald Angels Sing • It Came Upon the Midnight Clear • Jingle Bells • Joy to the World • O Christmas Tree • O Come, All Ye Faithful • O Holy Night • O Little Town of Bethlehem • Silent Night • Up on the Housetop.
00129248 .... $9.99

CHRISTMAS SONGS
Early Intermediate Level

The Chipmunk Song • The Christmas Song (Chestnuts Roasting on an Open Fire) • Do You Hear What I Hear • Feliz Navidad • Frosty the Snow Man • Have Yourself a Merry Little Christmas • Here Comes Santa Claus (Right Down Santa Claus Lane) • A Holly Jolly Christmas • (There's No Place Like) Home for the Holidays • Jingle Bell Rock • The Little Drummer Boy • Merry Christmas, Darling • The Most Wonderful Time of the Year • Silver Bells • White Christmas.
00129247 .... $9.99

CLASSIC ROCK
Mid-Intermediate Level

Aqualung • Behind Blue Eyes • Born to Be Wild • Crazy Train • Fly Like an Eagle • Free Bird • Hey Jude • Low Rider • Moondance • Oye Como Va • Proud Mary • (I Can't Get No) Satisfaction • Smoke on the Water • Summertime Blues • Sunshine of Your Love.
00103904 .... $9.99

HAWAIIAN SONGS
Mid-Intermediate Level

Aloha Oe • Beyond the Rainbow • Harbor Lights • Hawaiian War Chant (Ta-Hu-Wa-Hu-Wai) • The Hawaiian Wedding Song (Ke Kali Nei Au) • Ka-lu-a • Lovely Hula Hands • Mele Kalikimaka • The Moon of Manakoora • One Paddle, Two Paddle • Pearly Shells (Pupu 'O 'Ewa) • Red Sails in the Sunset • Sleepy Lagoon • Song of the Islands • Tiny Bubbles.
00119254 .... $9.99

THE NUTCRACKER
Late Intermediate Level

Arabian Dance ("Coffee") • Chinese Dance ("Tea") • Dance of the Reed-Flutes • Dance of the Sugar Plum Fairy • March • Overture • Russian Dance ("Trepak") • Waltz of the Flowers.
00119908 .... $9.99

ROCK INSTRUMENTALS
Late Intermediate Level

Beck's Bolero • Cissy Strut • Europa (Earth's Cry Heaven's Smile) • Frankenstein • Green Onions • Jessica • Misirlou • Perfidia • Pick Up the Pieces • Pipeline • Rebel 'Rouser • Sleepwalk • Tequila • Walk Don't Run • Wipe Out.
00103909 .... $9.99

STANDARDS & GEMS
Mid-Intermediate Level

Autumn Leaves • Cheek to Cheek • Easy to Love • Fly Me to the Moon • I Only Have Eyes for You • It Had to Be You • Laura • Mack the Knife • My Funny Valentine • Theme from "New York, New York" • Over the Rainbow • Satin Doll • Some Day My Prince Will Come • Summertime • The Way You Look Tonight.
00103898 .... $9.99

THEME MUSIC
Mid-Intermediate Level

Batman Theme • Theme from E.T. (The Extra-Terrestrial) • Forrest Gump – Main Title (Feather Theme) • The Godfather (Love Theme) • Hawaii Five-O Theme • He's a Pirate • Linus and Lucy • Mission: Impossible Theme • Peter Gunn • The Pink Panther • Raiders March • (Ghost) Riders in the Sky (A Cowboy Legend) • Theme from Spider Man • Theme from "Star Trek®" • Theme from "Superman."
00103903 .... $9.99

HAL•LEONARD®
CORPORATION
7777 W. BLUEMOUND RD. P.O. BOX 13819 MILWAUKEE, WI 53213

www.halleonard.com

UKULELE CHORD SONGBOOKS

This series features convenient 6" x 9" books with complete lyrics and chord symbols for dozens of great songs. Each song also includes chord grids at the top of every page and the first notes of the melody for easy reference.

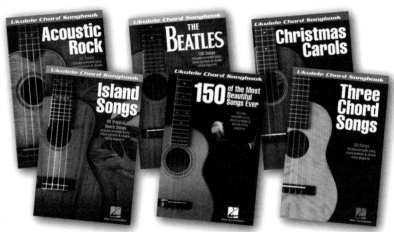

ACOUSTIC ROCK

60 tunes: American Pie • Band on the Run • Catch the Wind • Daydream • Every Rose Has Its Thorn • Hallelujah • Iris • More Than Words • Patience • The Sound of Silence • Space Oddity • Sweet Talkin' Woman • Wake up Little Susie • Who'll Stop the Rain • and more.
00702482 . . . . $14.99

THE BEATLES

100 favorites: Across the Universe • Carry That Weight • Dear Prudence • Good Day Sunshine • Here Comes the Sun • If I Fell • Love Me Do • Michelle • Ob-La-Di, Ob-La-Da • Revolution • Something • Ticket to Ride • We Can Work It Out • and many more.
00703065 . . . . $19.99

BEST SONGS EVER

70 songs: All I Ask of You • Bewitched • Edelweiss • Just the Way You Are • Let It Be • Memory • Moon River • Over the Rainbow • Someone to Watch over Me • Unchained Melody • You Are the Sunshine of My Life • You Raise Me Up • and more.
00117050 . . . . $16.99

CHILDREN'S SONGS

80 classics: Alphabet Song • "C" Is for Cookie • Do-Re-Mi • I'm Popeye the Sailor Man • Mickey Mouse March • Oh! Susanna • Polly Wolly Doodle • Puff the Magic Dragon • The Rainbow Connection • Sing • Three Little Fishies (Itty Bitty Poo) • and many more.
00702473 . . . . $14.99

CHRISTMAS CAROLS

75 favorites: Away in a Manger • Coventry Carol • The First Noel • Good King Wenceslas • Hark! the Herald Angels Sing • I Saw Three Ships • Joy to the World • O Little Town of Bethlehem • Still, Still, Still • Up on the Housetop • What Child Is This? • and more.
00702474 . . . . $14.99

CHRISTMAS SONGS

55 Christmas classics: Do They Know It's Christmas? • Frosty the Snow Man • Happy Xmas (War Is Over) • Jingle-Bell Rock • Little Saint Nick • The Most Wonderful Time of the Year • White Christmas • and more.
00101776 . . . . $14.99

ISLAND SONGS

60 beach party tunes: Blue Hawaii • Day-O (The Banana Boat Song) • Don't Worry, Be Happy • Island Girl • Kokomo • Lovely Hula Girl • Mele Kalikimaka • Red, Red Wine • Surfer Girl • Tiny Bubbles • Ukulele Lady • and many more.
00702471 . . . . $16.99

150 OF THE MOST BEAUTIFUL SONGS EVER

150 melodies: Always • Bewitched • Candle in the Wind • Endless Love • In the Still of the Night • Just the Way You Are • Memory • The Nearness of You • People • The Rainbow Connection • Smile • Unchained Melody • What a Wonderful World • Yesterday • and more.
00117051 . . . . $24.99

PETER, PAUL & MARY

Over 40 songs: And When I Die • Blowin' in the Wind • Goodnight, Irene • If I Had a Hammer (The Hammer Song) • Leaving on a Jet Plane • Puff the Magic Dragon • This Land Is Your Land • We Shall Overcome • Where Have All the Flowers Gone? • and more.
00121822 . . . . $12.99

THREE CHORD SONGS

60 songs: Bad Case of Loving You • Bang a Gong (Get It On) • Blue Suede Shoes • Cecilia • Get Back • Hound Dog • Kiss • Me and Bobby McGee • Not Fade Away • Rock This Town • Sweet Home Chicago • Twist and Shout • You Are My Sunshine • and more.
00702483 . . . . $14.99

TOP HITS

31 hits: The A Team • Born This Way • Forget You • Ho Hey • Jar of Hearts • Little Talks • Need You Now • Rolling in the Deep • Teenage Dream • Titanium • We Are Never Ever Getting Back Together • and more.
00115929 . . . . $14.99

HAL•LEONARD®
CORPORATION
7777 W. BLUEMOUND RD. P.O. BOX 13819 MILWAUKEE, WI 53213

www.halleonard.com

0814